12 Steps 12 Stories

Spiritual messages of recovery for children and the child in you.

D1569113

Debra Alessandra

12 Steps 12 Stories

Spiritual messages of recovery for children and the child in you.

by Debra Alessandra

Cover Design and Digital Illustrations by Kristin Staats

ISBN-13: 978-1492166719
ISBN-10: 1492166715

Original Twelve Steps as Published by Alcoholics Anonymous

1. We admitted we were powerless over alcohol—that our lives had become unmanageable.

2. Came to believe that a power greater than ourselves could restore us to sanity.

3. Made a decision to turn our will and our lives over to the care of God *as we understood Him*.

4. Made a searching and fearless moral inventory of ourselves.

5. Admitted to God, to ourselves, and to another human being the exact nature of our wrongs.

6. Were entirely ready to have God remove all these defects of character.

7. Humbly asked Him to remove our shortcomings.

8. Made a list of all persons we had harmed, and became willing to make amends to them all.

9. Made direct amends to such people wherever possible, except when to do so would injure them or others.

10. Continued to take personal inventory, and when we were wrong, promptly admitted it.

11. Sought through prayer and meditation to improve our conscious contact with God *as we understood Him*, praying only for knowledge of His will for us and the power to carry that out.

12. Having had a spiritual awakening as the result of these steps, we tried to carry this message to alcoholics, and to practice these principles in all our affairs.

Disclaimer

The Twelve Steps of Alcoholics Anonymous are reprinted and adapted with permission of Alcoholics Anonymous World Services, Inc. ("AAWS") Permission to adapt the Twelve Steps does not mean that AAWS has reviewed or approved the contents of this publication, or that AAWS necessarily agrees with the views expressed herein. A.A. is a program of recovery from alcoholism only - use of the Twelve Steps in connection with programs and activities which are patterned after A.A., but which address other problems, or in any other non-A.A. context, does not imply otherwise.

Dedication

I would like to extend my heartfelt thanks to my best friend Mary, who encouraged me to keep writing because her grandchildren needed these stories.

To Francis, whose guidance and direction has all too often saved my life.

To my love Tucker, who listened to me read my stories aloud until his ears fell off.

To my fellow writer and musician friend Kathy, who invited me to her writer's group and was the first person to say she loved my writer's voice.

To Frank, who was the first person to call me an author and regularly prodded me by asking how the stories were coming along.

To my dear friends Bud and Kathy, whose lives have clearly demonstrated these steps in action.

To Amy, Janie, Casey, and John, who were the first people I shared my project with and whose input I respect.

To my precious daughter, who appeared to learn these principles through osmosis and continues to be a great source of inspiration to me.

To my mother, who impacted my life on a level I will never adequately describe.

To my Higher Power, who orchestrated my life to this point and expresses through me as an instrument in his plans of Love.

May the light of love find a home in us all.

There is no spiritual part of life. It's all spiritual.

Author's Note

When Alcoholics Anonymous (AA) began, the world was a different place. I do not believe the founders of AA, Bill W. or Dr. Bob, could have envisioned the future as it is today. In 1935, the creation of the 12 Steps was unique to alcoholics, and the program and fellowship of Alcoholics Anonymous was a completely new approach to the disease of alcohol addiction. It is no wonder Bill Wilson was listed by *Time Magazine* as one of the top one-hundred most influential people of the last century. M. Scott Peck, author of *The Road Less Traveled*, refers to the creation of AA as the greatest positive event in the twentieth century.

There are two key concepts I would like to address with regards to my body of work. The first is my exclusive use of the words alcoholic and alcoholism. Although AA is specifically for those who have a desire to stop drinking, over four-hundred other fellowships have asked and received permission to use the 12 Step Recovery Format to address their needs. Just as other groups utilize the 12 Step Recovery Process, please know that when I refer to alcoholics, you may feel free to substitute any number of words to address your particular circumstance or addiction problem to which the 12 Steps will apply. The worldwide explosion of self-help groups that use the same 12 Steps has proven the effectiveness of this approach to healing those afflicted with other addictions. The success of the 12 Step Process in the fellowship of AA has shone like a beacon in the dark, heralding a way to recover for others suffering from any number of forms of addiction.

The second area of clarification that I'd like to address is my use of the word God. When Alcoholics Anonymous emerged and blossomed into groups across the United States, the fellowship frequently relied on two phrases to describe a Power Greater than oneself. In all AA literature, the words Higher Power and God were commonly used. With the resulting flourish of AA worldwide and the multiple offshoots, it is significant to note that the 'nature' of the steps holds all-inclusive across cultures. People of all faiths, religions, and even lack of religion have felt free to implement their perception of God. Many people have found comfort in other descriptive words: One Who Has All Power, God as You Understand God, Creative Intelligence, Universal Mind, Spirit of Nature, and Source. These are just a few of the descriptive words people use. Therefore, please realize your own perception of God is sufficient to open the door to a new way of life; a spiritual design for living. Let no language barriers interfere with your embrace of the fundamental formula for release from the grip of addiction.

Contents

Contents

For Children

Someone you love has a disease called alcoholism. They didn't choose to be an alcoholic. They didn't wish it upon themselves or the ones they love. Perhaps you didn't know much about their disease and neither did they. Like many diseases, it gets worse over time instead of better. Please know that you are not alone. Many children are in the very same situation as you are. They number in the millions.

Living with an alcoholic hurts. Maybe you have felt scared or angry. Being in the dark about this disease may be confusing or upsetting. Often you can see how bad things are long before the alcoholic will see it for themselves. Usually you wish they would stop long before they do. Unfortunately, they have to sink so low, that they want to stop drinking. Then something wonderful happens. A journey of recovery begins.

The topic of recovery might be confusing as well. These stories will help you understand what your loved one is doing at those recovery meetings and why the meetings are so important to them.

All my characters in the stories learn something about themselves and the world by taking certain steps. No doubt you've heard those words in your home. The steps help a person get better. When you finish reading, you too, will know a thing or two about the steps.

About the Disease

Alcoholism is a disease that has three parts. It effects a person's mind, body, and spirit. People use big words to tell about this condition. They explain the condition as an obsession to mean the person can't stop thinking about their next drink even when it leads to trouble. They say it is an allergy of the body which means they react differently to alcohol than people without the disease. While some people can have one or two drinks and put them down, an alcoholic can't seem to get enough once they start drinking. Alcoholism is a bankruptcy of the spirit. This means the alcoholic has lost their connection to a Power Greater than themselves.

About Recovery

When an alcoholic wants to stop drinking, their lives can improve. One way they can stop drinking and stay stopped is to attend meetings of Alcoholics Anonymous. There they are often told a way to solve their drinking problem. Usually they feel better when they are with other alcoholics who are working the program with them.

If being sober is important to them, they will try to use the solutions that others are using. There are twelve solutions. They are called steps. Like a stairway, they are a way up and out of the disease of alcoholism. When practiced as a way of life, they may not return to drinking.

These twelve stories will help you understand the twelve steps of the program someone you love is trying to live by. People who are not alcoholics may read these steps, think they sound good, but not really practice them in their lives. An alcoholic can stay away from a drink one day at a time, if they grow their spiritual life and practice using these steps.

For Parents

"Freedom makes a huge requirement of every human being. With freedom comes responsibility."- Eleanor Roosevelt

Utilizing the 12 steps and attempting to apply them in your life is an ongoing learning experience. One must work each day to maintain sobriety. One day at a time an alcoholic learns to develop and nurture their spiritual life. They learn to become productive members of society, a friend among friends, and a person of good character.

Many alcoholics are good at minimizing the impact the disease had on the younger members in their family. They blindly hope their sobriety is enough to mend the pain. But truth be told, deep down, they realize there is more work to be done in order to repair the damage their alcoholism inflicted.

Often they try to convince themselves that children are too young to approach. At times, they are at a loss for words to explain the disease to their children. The challenge of this issue is considerable. Yes, children do need help. Their needs are three-fold.

First, you can provide them with information about alcoholism. There are many valuable books and materials that are available. (See Page 96) Children thrive on information that speaks to their experience and helps them make sense of their concerns.

Secondly, children need a safe place to express their feelings. A loving environment, coupled with opportunities to feel their feelings without constraint, opens a way for healing to occur. Many family therapists, counselors, and community groups encourage and allow for children to be heard as part of their healing process.

A number of resources can provide assistance. Your child's teacher, guidance counselor, after-care provider, minister, social worker, and grandparents are just a few examples.

Finally, children need an understanding of the basic components of recovery. Alcoholics may find explaining their new recovery based lifestyle difficult. Even good changes require effort. Try answering the following questions. How can you allow children to feel included and be informed? How can the journey of the 12 Step Recovery be explained?

As stated by NACoA, "Total family recovery requires total family effort." Yes, explore the available resources in your community and within your area of the world, but without a doubt, the most valuable resource they need is you. Children need your time and attention. A little goes a long way.

These stories will open the door to a deeper relationship with the children you love. May today mark a new beginning as you share in the simplicity and deeper meaning of each story. May you savor the messages and use them as a platform from which you dive deeper into health, healing, and wholeness. May they help the children you love feel comforted, included, and valued.

Step One
We admitted we were powerless and our lives had become unmanageable.

Edd, the dog, lived on a very busy street. He loved to watch the cars whiz by. His family trained him to stay in the yard. One day he thought, "I wonder if I can make it across the street?" He had no idea how this simple question would change his whole life. Even though he knew the danger, he thought, "I can do it."

Off he ran.

Perhaps it was a touch of defiance or maybe the thrill of something new. "This sure is exciting!" he panted when he reached the other side.

That night as he lay in his dog bed, Edd felt better than ever. He grinned as only a dog can, "This is fantastic!" He tried to convince himself that it was okay. "Heck, all dogs run across the street sometimes. Why not me?"

Sneaking behind his owners' backs added to his delight. "I don't think I belong with this family anyway," Edd secretly thought. Before long he snuck out again. And then again.

Each and every time Edd dodged through the cars, he felt a rush of excitement. "I think I've found the one thing in my life I've been missing," he told himself.

Over time, Edd's habit took a turn for the worse. His owners found out Edd *loved* darting across the street. At first they made excuses for him, just like he had done for himself, but deep down they were troubled.

His family scolded Edd and said, "Stop that!" and "No!" They put up fences. They wanted to protect him but nothing they tried seemed to work. Somehow he would dig under the fence and escape. Edd was unstoppable.

"What are we going to do?" they asked each other. They were at their wit's end.

One morning, Edd heard a horn blast and brakes squeal. He felt a tire scrape down his side. Bruised and upset, he wandered home. "I'm going to quit this running across the street business," he promised himself. "It's not much fun anymore. In fact, it seems downright dangerous."

However as time would have it, in a day or two, he usually felt as good as new.

Little by little things got worse. In his quiet time, before he drifted off to sleep, he wondered about his habit. He thought, "This is more dangerous than I ever imagined." But he quickly dismissed that thought.

"I'm okay now," he convinced himself. But he was wrong.

The day the vet put a cast on his broken leg, he swore he'd quit running across the street forever. In the doctor's office, his family talked about him like he wasn't even in the room. "We can't seem to stop him," they complained.

"You know, it's only a matter of time until Edd breaks his back or worse… gets killed by a car," he overheard the vet say.

Edd was puzzled. "How am I going to stop? If I lose my legs, I will never grow new ones!" he worried.

18

While his leg was getting better, he had more time to think about his life. "What is wrong with me?" he asked himself. He noticed the other dogs. They stayed in their yards without needing to escape. He thought, "Why, they're not getting hurt." He wished he could be like them.

With great determination, Edd came up with lots of good ideas. "I'm going to swear off running between cars forever." But before the cast had even been removed, he'd made a new plan.

Each time he took a solemn oath and made a promise to himself. "I'm only going to run across the street once a day." More ideas came. "I will run when my family is not home. Maybe if I run late at night, no one will ever find out." Over and over again Edd tried to convince himself he might learn to control his habit and enjoy himself like the first time. He believed, "If I can follow these rules, everything will be fine."

Although Edd would do well for a while, he always found himself getting into trouble again. "Why is it so hard to stop?" he asked himself. A small voice inside his head called to him and whispered, "Come on Edd, it'll make you feel better." And then Edd could not resist.

The last time Edd scurried across the street was indeed his last, although he didn't know it at the time.

A huge garbage truck came barreling down the road. He barely escaped being crushed beneath its huge wheels. The force threw him into a ditch. While lying on the side of the road, he thought his heart would burst. He was full of fear and shame. Edd felt defeated.

He limped all the way home and laid alone on the front porch.

He whined softly and whimpered, "God help me." Anyone would agree, Edd needed a miracle.

Edd finally admitted he was completely powerless and he could not manage his own life.

Now Edd knew that it was true.

Step One Follow-Up

We all have habits. Some are good for us and improve our lives like brushing our teeth or reading a story before bedtime. Sometimes they are not good for us like picking a scab or grinding our teeth.

• Have you ever had a habit you could not stop? Maybe it was as simple as sucking your thumb or biting your fingernails.

_____

_____

_____

_____

Edd's habit was more serious than thumb sucking or nail biting. Even though he tried to manage it, he could not. It could have cost him his life.

When an alcoholic wants to stop drinking, it can be difficult. Like Edd, his habit has become quite hard to control. It has grown into an addiction.

An alcoholic has a disease that makes him want to drink even

though it causes him problems. He says he wants to stop, but he does not always stay stopped.

• Have you seen this in someone you care about?

_____

- -

_____

_____

- -

_____

• Can you remember something you did to keep them from drinking?

_____

- -

_____

_____

- -

_____

Only the alcoholic can get honest with themselves. They must admit they are powerless and they need help. Then their life can begin to change for the better.

Step Two
Came to believe that a power greater than ourselves could restore us to sanity.

Carmen sat in his desk at school. Mrs. Henry was good at asking questions. This morning he was extra good at listening.

His third grade teacher asked, "Who can tell about a time when people changed what they believed?" The class fell quiet. They all thought hard.

Finally, Noah raised his hand and said, "Well, people believed the world was flat for a long time. They were afraid to travel too far. They thought they might fall off the edge of the earth."

Ruby added, "They also believed the earth was the center of the universe. People would boast that they were quite certain that everything revolved around them. They never imagined they were traveling around the sun."

"Oh wait, I know one more," Iris exclaimed. "People used to say if God wanted men to fly, He would have given them wings. Now airplanes are as common as cars."

"Sometimes an idea that seems true is replaced," Mrs. Henry explained. "It gets thrown in the trash with the other old ideas because it no longer makes good sense."

Carmen was quite curious. For some strange reason, this was a lesson Carmen did not forget. "I wonder if this might happen to me in my lifetime?" he thought.

Carmen grew into a man and like those before him, Carmen believed in things that were not true. They actually seemed quite sane at the time. People had told him to have faith in a Higher Power. "That's fine for them," he thought. But he never really let this Power into his own life. He was too busy playing the big shot.

Carmen thought, "There is no power greater than me." He loved to say, "I can do it myself." His mind was bright. His willpower was strong. "This is a race I'm sure to win," he thought to himself.

One summer day, Carmen changed his ideas about a Higher Power. He found it necessary in order to go on. It was a day he would never forget. During the annual Race for Humanity, Carmen fell to his knees. He knew something had been terribly wrong for quite some time but he pretended he was okay. "I'm fine," he told the others.

Although usually swift and steady, Carmen lagged behind. "Which way am I going?" he worried. He had left the others and was separated from the pack. He sensed he was lost yet he continued running. "I know I'm going to win!" he panted and tried to convince himself. "I'll bet I've found a better way."

He was shocked when he came to the end of the road. "How could there be a deadend in the race?" he asked. His mind was spinning. His muscles cramped into knots. "My lungs feel like they're on fire!" he cried. Carmen was confused. His heart raced. His whole body ached. But the pain in his soul was the greatest of all.

Carmen was lost and afraid. "How can it be that all my hard work has failed me?" he wondered. "I've always been so good at racing."

"Geez, my scorecard might read zero!" he fretted. Carmen felt hopeless.

It was not long before his friend Leo came to his side. He talked to Carmen with kind and soothing words. They made him feel more hopeful.

Leo explained, "Carmen, if you could believe like I do, believe in a Spirit of the Universe or a Power Greater than yourself, your life would change."

"I know how it feels to be hopeless," Leo confided. "You will find a new peace and happiness if you give it a try. You might figure out which direction to go."

Leo continued, "Others have solved their problems by relying upon a Power Greater than themselves." "I've watched it work for them," Leo assured him. "And, it's worked for me!"

Carmen thought, "Possibly, just possibly, there *is* something greater than I am."

"Any words will do," Leo told him. "You can have faith in whatever Power you need, as long as you don't rely only on your own power."

"It makes sense, but I'm just not sure," Carmen hesitated. During his pause, he remembered back to Mrs. Henry and her important lesson. "Maybe *I can* change?" he felt a shift inside. "Maybe I'm clinging to an old idea."

When Carmen became willing to believe, his whole body, mind, and soul began to relax. He looked at Leo and sighed, "Ah, there, I think I feel the change already."

He had taken a small but mighty step forward on a new path. With only a tiny amount of faith, his new journey began. "Am I heading toward a new and better life?"

"Yes," Leo assured him. "You are on your way."

Like the lesson he'd learned in school, Carmen knew it was time to let go of his old ideas.

And Leo encouraged him more. "Over time you will feel even more joy and happiness and peace, Carmen. You can trust that."

The simple change of believing in a Power Greater than himself held the key.

Now Carmen knew that it was true.

Carmen had some ideas that didn't really help his life go smoothly. He thought he could do everything by himself. He thought he knew what was best and how to win at the game of life. He was mistaken.

• Did you ever think you were doing something right and found out it was wrong? (Maybe you were sure the number thirteen was an unlucky number and then you found out it was not.)

_____

_ _

_____

_____

_ _

_____

Carmen believed that he knew his way, but he got lost. Part of his problem was he only had faith in himself. Life had to get pretty hard for him to let go of his old ideas.

• Do you understand that believing in a Power Greater than yourself will help you have a better life? That Power can be called different names. Spirit of the Universe, Great Reality, and God are just a few.

_____

_ _

_____

_____

_ _

Like Carmen, alcoholics have to believe in a Power Greater than themselves. Even if at first they are not sure, they have to be willing to have faith. They must try this in order to recover from their alcoholism. Being willing to believe is the key that opens the door to a happier life.

• Does anyone you know have this willingness?

_____

_ _

_____

_____

_ _

_____

• How can you tell?

_____

_ _

_____

_____

_ _

_____

Step Three
Made a decision to turn our will and our lives over to the care of God.

Chloe was a soft grey tabby cat. She lived with a whole litter of kittens and in a happy home. She was like most cats in some ways, but exceptional in other ways. She took great pride in being able to take care of herself, without anyone's help. Chloe often said, "I don't need anyone to tell me what to do or how to do it."

Her owners called her a fancy name. They called her "self-sufficient."

Chloe liked the feeling of control. She liked playing God. In the beginning, it worked well.

Chloe's self-sufficiency began when she was just a kitten. She thought, "I will sleep whenever I feel like it. I will ignore my owners when they call me by name."

She pranced around the house with her nose held high. She looked confident from the outside, but on the inside Chloe was more than a little scared and even a bit lonely. After a while, she became angry too. As these feelings grew, so did her attempts to control others. The truth was, she wasn't really comfortable in her own fur.

During playtime, she would act like she was in charge. She would meow her orders. People could hear her from the next room saying to the other cats, "You scratch right here," or "No, purr like this." Chloe acted sassy and bossed them some more. "Oh no, that will never do….take your nap over there."

While scratching her claws on her special scratching post she'd think, "Am I the only one who sees how this should be?"

At first her kitten friends would play along with her demanding ways. They would do as they were told. This suited Chloe's plans just fine.

But her happy feelings never seemed to last very long. It was hard to keep everybody in line. Chloe would give them orders. If they didn't do as she said, she would get quite upset. "What is wrong with these cats?" her mind raced. "Why can't they all just listen to me?" There was no pleasing Chloe.

Her friends and family heard, "I am right, and you are wrong" one time too many! They knew they would never be perfect. They were doing the best that they could. Eventually, they stopped trying to please Chloe and started living their own lives.

Nobody meant to upset Chloe. However, she got plenty upset. Alone and confused, she wondered, "Will I ever be happy…really happy?"

Chloe kept on trying to live by her own will. She was getting older and may have gone on being her bossy self to the bitter end, but one day a miracle occurred. And she didn't even plan it herself.

Chloe's friend Logan could tell that she was in pain. He wanted to help her see that her life could be different, that she could find a little peace.

Logan said, "If you make a decision to stop trying to be in charge of everyone…if you stop playing God, your life can change. You can start to grow in new ways and you will feel moments of joy. All you have to do is make that decision."

"Stop trying to control everything and everyone," Logan continued. "You know Chloe, if you would just make this decision, all sorts of wonderful things will happen for you."

"Well, I'm hurting enough to give it a try," she admitted.

Right then and there, Chloe decided to give up trying to be in charge all the time. She began to trust that God would care for her and everything was the way it was meant to be. Chloe was willing and able to make this decision.

Making the decision to turn her will and her life over to the care of God was the proper use of her willpower.

Now Chloe knew that it was true.

Chloe liked to think she was in charge. She kept arranging her fellow cats like they were actors on a stage. She pushed and prodded and tried to control them. She never realized the only cat she could control was herself. She thought everything should go her way. And she liked doing what she wanted whenever she wanted. Chloe was what people call 'self-sufficient'. That means you do everything yourself. Sometimes this leads to unhappiness. It pushes others away.

• Did you ever try to do everything yourself?

_____

_ _

_____

_____

_ _

_____

• Have you ever been upset when people do not behave the way *you* want?

_____

_ _

_____

_____

_ _

_____

An alcoholic has to trust that he can turn his will and life over to the care of God. Like a baby has to trust his mother, alcoholics must decide to trust God. It's hard to tell if an alcoholic has made this decision. Over time, you will notice the change. Maybe it will feel better to be in their company.

Step Four
Made a searching and fearless moral inventory of ourselves.

Jonathan was a special goldfish. He loved to swim and eat. But even more than that, he loved to talk and think.

He glided around in his great, big tank with all of the other fish. As he talked, his words formed tiny bubbles. He chattered with pride, "I like to think of questions and then answer them all by myself!" Even though his brain was small, no question was too hard when he put his mind to the task at hand.

He asked himself, "What is two plus two?" He knew the answer. He had already solved the problem with his little fish pencil. He kept one tucked behind his fin for times just like this.

He asked himself, "What color is the water?" He knew that answer, too. The other fish were tricked, and thought it was blue, but not Jonathan. He could tell the water wasn't blue. "I cannot be fooled," he splashed with delight. He realized the gravel on the bottom only made the water look blue and announced, "The water is actually clear."

Jonathan felt ordinary, but the other fish marveled and said, "You're so smart!"

One day, Jonathan swam around the tank admiring the other fish. He smiled when he glimpsed at the yellow ones with shiny, blue spots. Some even had big angel fins. Others had stripes. He especially liked the tiny, bright red fish.

Jonathan thought of a new question that he had never thought of before. "What's in the middle of them?" Then he gulped. "Better yet, what's in the middle of me?"

He did not know this answer and that worried him. Never before had Jonathan been so stumped. "Hmm," he gurgled. "I wonder if we're as lovely on the inside as we look on the outside?"

"Gosh," he exclaimed. "I wish I hadn't thought of this question. What if I find a yucky, green monster or a slimy, dark thing? What if I find spooky sounds and awful smells?" Jonathan twitched as a tingling shiver raced up his spine.

"Wait a minute!" he continued. "I've heard of muscles and a stomach. I know I have a bony spine. Surely I have a heart, but I'll bet I have much more."

Jonathan boldly declared, "I will find the answer, no matter what it takes," because if the truth be told, he had never asked himself a more important question before.

Jonathan turned his eyes inward to have a look. At first, he saw nothing. His middle was hidden beneath a pile of memories. "Let me get to the bottom of this," Jonathan said, searching bravely. "I can see clearly through my good memories, but the bad memories make my insides quite cloudy."

He exclaimed, "Are my bad memories clouding up the view?"

Jonathan wondered, "What can I do?" but he carried on with his mission. "I must search for the truth about myself." He made a plan to write down all of his memories, in hopes that it would help him find what he was looking for.

"I'll use my special fish paper and pencil for something this important," he decided. "Writing is hard for me, but I will do it." He slipped the paper from under a rock and began to swirl. Each word took effort.

Once he began to write, he felt brave and strong. He wrote down everything he could remember. Memories and secrets that were tucked deep down inside, soon rose into his mind like bubbles to the surface of the water.

"I remember the time I snatched dinner from my friend Claude." He felt guilty. "Yes, and then there was the time I swam right by my friend who was in danger and all I worried about was what might have happened to me." He saw how selfish he had been.

Jonathan had sad memories, too. One day he and his sister had been darting through the plastic castles, alive and happy. The next day, she was floating in the tank, never able to keep him company again. He whispered sadly, "I'm still not sure what happened to her."

Finally he finished his search and saw all the way deep inside of himself.

"What a delightful surprise! Oh my, it looks like a pearl!" he thought. He saw a hundred shades of pink and blue and brown, each layer more colorful than the last. Deep down, his middle shimmered with a soft and special glow. No yucky green monster or creepy slime clung to his middle. No spooky sounds or awful smells lingered inside. It was a beautiful pearl!

Jonathan gazed at his special jewel with love. "It might take work, but I will do what I need to in order to keep my middle clear and shining," he promised himself. "I don't want these bad feelings to pile up ever again!"

After searching deep inside himself, Jonathan knew the answer to his question. He felt much better. Under all the memories, deep in his middle, something beautiful lived.

Now Jonathan knew that it was true.

Step Four Follow-Up

Jonathan had to answer some hard questions.

• Have you ever had to put in a lot of effort to find an answer?

_____

_ _

_____

_____

_ _

_____

Jonathan had to look inside himself and uncover feelings that were bothering him. It took courage to write about the emotions that he would rather forget.

• Do you hide your feelings? How do you think you could work on revealing things that bother you?

_____

_ _

_____

_____

_ _

_____

Jonathan had to go on a fact-finding mission and take inventory of his feelings. It's important to see what is working and discard what is not. He had to get rid of these items without regret. If an alcoholic does not take inventory, he may return to drinking.

• How does holding a secret make you feel?

_____

_____

_____

_____

Step Five
Admitted to God, to ourselves, and another human being the exact nature of our wrongs.

The rain finally stopped and the sun peeked through the clouds. One of God's miracles spread across the sky. "Oh my, it's a rainbow," Benjamin the bear noticed as he lumbered out of his cave. He squinted at the sun. "I sure have been inside a long time."

Benjamin had been thinking and writing. He had been looking for the truth about himself. "I'm pretty certain I've found it," he said to himself.

He put these writings and thoughts in a pot…his special magic pot. Sometimes his pot seemed very small and sometimes quite large. It changed often. "Today it's so large, I can't carry it alone," Benjamin knew. He was used to doing everything by himself. He found it hard to ask for help.

He sat down on the grass to admire the rainbow. "I wonder if it is okay to tell anyone. Will others run away if they know the truth?" Some of his truths were private and some were embarrassing. Benjamin was not proud of himself, but the rainbow held a promise.

"Maybe God already knows what's in my pot and what I've been keeping to myself," he wondered. "I guess it's possible," Benjamin decided. "But I'll tell him anyway." He believed his God cared about him and would help him become the best bear he could be. This was the whole reason he wrote and thought so hard in the first place.

He pulled his writings out of the pot one by one and read them to

God. When he felt sad he cried. He shook when he felt scared. He pounded his paw to the ground when he felt angry. As he finished, the magic pot turned to gold…sparkling and shining bright. He felt a lot better.

"Wait a minute," he remembered. "I must do more."

He lay back on the ground, closed his eyes and waited. It seemed he had only been there for a moment when he felt a soft paw on the side of his face. It was gentle and kind. His friend Jacob stood close by. Jacob and Benjamin were rather new friends, but they had a lot in common.

"Will you help me?" Benjamin asked Jacob. "Of course," Jacob answered. Together they carried the magic gold pot toward the end of the rainbow. Then Benjamin told Jacob about everything in his pot, even his secrets. They talked for a long time and he held nothing back.

When Benjamin finished, Jacob spoke to his dear and wonderful friend. He said, "In the whole world, there is only one you. No one else looks quite the way you do or thinks and acts the way you do. You are a brave bear and you have done a wonderful thing."

Jacob continued. "When you share yourself, I see not only a pearl…but look," he pointed to the pot, brimming with jewels: rubies and emeralds, sapphires and diamonds.

"Magnificent!" Jacob exclaimed.

Benjamin was not sure what magnificent meant, but it felt good. He had a feeling of belonging that he hadn't felt before.

Jacob said, "Benjamin, I want you to lift the pot and bring it close to your chest. Now close your eyes and let the pot go."

The magic pot, full of truths about Benjamin, slowly floated away and disappeared. "You can forgive yourself," Jacob assured him. "Let it go."

Benjamin sighed with relief. No more fooling himself. No more pretending. He could see the truth about himself because he had written everything down and he had shared it with God and his new friend. He softly repeated Jacob's words. "You are a brave bear and you have done a great thing."

Now Benjamin knew that this was true.

Step Five Follow-Up

They say a problem shared is a problem that's been cut in half.
Benjamin had to look way down deep inside to find the cause of
his problems. He shared his 'inventory' with God and another bear.
He had to look at what was good and what was not so good about
himself. He had to be open and honest. This is not always easy.

• Have you ever wanted to talk to someone about your feelings but
  held back?

_____

_____

_____

_____

• Have you been afraid maybe others wouldn't like you if you told
  on yourself?

_____

_____

_____

_____

Alcoholics have to talk to another human being. They have to tell on themselves. They have to talk about things they might rather keep buried inside. If they hold anything back, they may drink again. The very thing they don't want to share may be a trigger to return to drinking. Luckily for Benjamin he trusted a loving God who wanted only his highest and best. He found a friend that accepted him just as he was. His friend helped him see himself more clearly and brought him great relief.

• Do you have a friend or relative you can talk to?

_____

_____

_____

_____

• Do you feel safe when you confide in them?

_____

_____

_____

_____

Step Six
Were entirely ready to have God remove all these defects of character.

Willie was a very special car. He was bright red with silver stripes. More than anything else, Willie loved parades. His heart skipped a beat at the very thought of them. He liked the twirling batons and the deep bass drums. Better yet, he enjoyed the colorful balloons, candy, and confetti. He was so excited to hear that a new parade was coming to town.

"Oh, boy!" exclaimed Willie. "How shall I get ready?"

One night, Willie was settling down to sleep and, of course, thinking about the parade. "I hope I get to be in the parade," he sighed. Willie stretched his headlights extra wide to see how he looked. He knew that he had to look his best. "Gee, I'm clean in some places, but I can't see all of me. I'll bet there is more work to be done."

Although Willie loved taking care of himself, he couldn't do some of the clean-up because he couldn't reach some areas. "How can I polish my chrome or shine my lights? I can't even see all that needs to be done. Is my rear bumper rusty?" he worried. "Are any of my windows cracked?"

His dear friend Tommy the tow truck, pulled up by the garage where Willie lived. Tommy tried to help Willie see some of his faults, but everything was not clear right away. Willie searched his memory for the reasons he had some of these flaws.

He thought about the deep scratch on his hood. "Oh, that happened during a storm when a tree branch fell on me," Willie admitted. He was actually quite proud he had managed to move out from under the branch by his own power. The scratch occurred when he decided to exert himself. Willie marveled at this accomplishment.

"Does it really need to be removed?" he winced.

"Maybe I can pick and choose what seems right to me," he thought. But, somehow that did not seem correct.

Willie was used to relying on himself. But in the middle of that very night, he realized he needed to be ready to rely on something more powerful than himself. A lot of people called that something, God.

"Am I ready to quit acting like I always know what to do? Do I have the courage to ask for help fixing myself up?" All of these questions swirled around in his mind.

Tommy had told him, "If you will allow Him to, God can help you do what you cannot do all by yourself." Willie thought he was ready to stop trying to fix all of his own problems. He was ready to have faith and leave it to God.

"If I want to be the best that I can be, I know I have to be ready for God to work in my life. Just talking about it, won't work. Just thinking about it, won't work either," he reminded himself. "If I really want to be in this parade, I should let go and let God."

"I know that being ready is only a beginning, but it's a mighty good start!" He raised his headlights and looked toward the sky. "Only God is perfect. But I can move in that direction too," he rumbled his engine. God knew what Willie needed. He also knew how to help him be his brightest and best. His engine purred. He was thrilled with the possibility.

The following day, a friendly mechanic named Mac arrived to work on Willie. "Mac must be a gift from God," Willie thought. Mac brought buckets of water, soap, and wax. He took out his oilcan and special tools. Willie overheard Mac wishing under his breath, "I'd sure like to drive *this* car in the parade!"

"What fun!" Willie grinned, "Yes, being ready is a good start!" Willie felt certain that with God's help, he would be in the parade.

Now Willie knew that it was true.

Step Six Follow-Up

Willie could not see all of himself very clearly. He needed some help from his friend Tommy Tow Truck.

• Do you find you need some help to see yourself?

_____

_____

_____

_____

• Has anyone ever told you something about yourself you hadn't really noticed?

_____

_____

_____

_____

An alcoholic has to be willing to accept his defects. He has to be willing to let his defects go in order to change. This is the step where he allows new and better things to come into his life. Willie had to stop trying to fix himself without God's help.

Before you do something important you have to get ready, just like an athlete before a big game.

• Can you name a time you spent getting ready for something important?

_____

_ _

_____

_ _

_____

To be the best that they can be, alcoholics have to be ready to have God work in their life.

• Do you think you can turn to God for help?

_____

_ _

_____

Step Seven
Humbly asked Him to remove our shortcomings.

Francis lived in a cozy little area in the corner of Elijah's backyard. She croaked with glee as the evening sun went down. She liked hiding under the ferns and singing in the rain. Other frogs lived nearby. "Life is good and I like it here," she exclaimed.

Life had not always been this good. At one time, Francis had been full of fear. Even though most frogs can see forward, sideways, and upward all at the same time, she had been shortsighted and worst of all, she was demanding.

Since coming to Elijah's house, Francis felt better than she ever had before. Her skin was moist. She had plenty of bugs to snack on. A new peace entered her heart and pushed away the fear she used to live with everyday.

Elijah made her feel right at home. He loved Francis beyond words. "I only want what is best for you," he often told her. Francis felt comfortable and safe in his presence.

One day, Elijah wanted to build a shed in the exact spot where Francis felt the happiest. She was snuggled in under the leaves by the pond when Elijah asked, "Francis, will you move over so I can build a shed?" Francis heard him saying how much better it would be. Better for the both of them.

"No, please, no!" Francis begged and dug a bit deeper into the mud.

A struggle began to stir inside of Francis. She puffed up her frog cheeks and pouted. "Why do I have to change?" she wondered. "I'd rather stay right here!"

Francis wrestled with the feelings inside herself for quite some time. "I like it here," she repeated over and over.

But then she remembered how she had lived before. "This is so much better," she reminded herself. "Elijah protects and cares for me."

She thought of all the times in the past when he had helped her. Francis remembered the awful day when she lay trapped in the bottom of the huge flowerpot. Even with her strong back legs, Francis knew she would never escape. Francis felt defeated. Elijah came and gently lifted her out. "Ah, there, that's much better," she thought. What a relief!

Before that, Francis had thought living by the side of the road was the best she was ever going to get. She had always been disturbed by the loud traffic and frustrated by how hard life was for her. The loud traffic gave her a headache and her stomach churned with hunger.

When Elijah brought her home, he promised that he would take care of her and that she could trust him completely. That memory brought peace to Francis' mind.

Francis gripped her legs together to pray and a part of her anger let go. She let go of all the wrestling inside and thought, "Even though I don't want to move, I don't always know what's best for me. And who knows, maybe I can be useful to him for once. I could even help the other frogs, too!"

Francis prayed, "God, please take away my weaknesses!" Then she agreed to move over so Elijah could build a shed. She had no reason not to trust him completely. Francis now believed with all her heart that Elijah knew what was in her best interest.

By asking God to take away her weaknesses, she relaxed even more. "Maybe my new place will be even better than my old one!"

Now Francis knew that it was true.

Step Seven Follow-Up

A shortcoming is a flaw or a weak point. Francis' weak point was her fear of change. Sometimes people are afraid to change, but change may improve their lives.

• What do you think made Francis want to stay in the same place?

_____

_____

_____

_____

_____

• Did you ever fight doing something and then find out the very thing you resisted was better than anything you could have planned?

_____

_____

_____

_____

_____

It took some effort, but with God's help, Francis finally trusted Elijah enough to allow him to work in her life. What seemed like a bad thing may actually be quite good.

• Do you think Francis will enjoy her new home?

_____

_____

_____

_____

Alcoholics have to ask for their shortcomings to be removed. Alcoholics have to trust God, like Francis had to trust Elijah.

• Would you have trusted Elijah?

_____

_____

_____

_____

Step Eight
Made a list of all people we had harmed and became willing to make amends to them all.

Billy was a pencil, just one pencil among many others. Still, in his heart, he knew he wasn't like just any ordinary pencil. He felt like he was one-of-a-kind, but not in a good way.

"I know what it's like to have my point snapped off, my sides chewed, and my eraser totally smudged. He believed few of his pencil friends had been through the tough times that he had. In Billy's little mind, his life was hard.

Billy lived in a pencil can with others. Some were colored. Green and blue were two of his favorites. Fancy pens joined the mix. Most pencils were plain and yellow on the outside with a shiny gold collar and soft pink eraser.

The pens said, "We're good for letter writing." The colored pencils boasted, "We're best for drawing." The regular pencils had their place, too. Billy did crossword puzzles and math with the best of them. And he was good at making lists.

"Lists are helpful," Billy bragged. "A list keeps me from forgetting things."

So, one day Billy made a list unlike any other. "I've made lists before, but none as important as this one," he realized. This list had names of others on it, mostly close friends and family. This list was good for more than just remembering. "This list will open up more space in my life for love and joy and real happiness." Billy felt it right to his lead core.

His friend Charlie told him, "Billy, you have to be willing to go to each pencil or pen on the list and fix any trouble between you and them." Charlie explained, "Yes, sometimes your feelings got hurt, but what we need to examine is *your* part in the trouble."

Billy looked back at the difficult times with friends and family to see *his* part in them. "Hmm," he thought, "What have *I* done to hurt them?"

He remembered when the colored pencils were being used, the can felt roomy. But after making a map or a picture, they'd come back. Sometimes their points would scrape his side. "Boy, did I get mad," he remembered. "And just to show how mad I was, I would squeeze against them when they returned." Instead of allowing them back in, he would press his skinny body against the side of the can to keep them out. "Not only did it hurt me, I know it hurt them, too," Billy realized.

As Billy pushed against the colored pencils, his point got dull or his eraser head smudged against the bottom of the can. No matter if he was doing a headstand or standing upright, he was sore. Plus, it felt cold against the side of the can. He only thought about himself. All day long thoughts of me, me, me ran his life.

Before Billy made his list, being angry was as far as he usually got. He knew his feelings had to change. "Now, I'm trying to live in a new way. Living with a cold and tight heart is no fun at all."

Billy had a new goal. He was trying to get rid of his selfish habits. His head was clear. "I can tell my friends I am sorry now."

But that was only a start. Just saying, "I'm sorry" is not enough. It was important to take the next step. "I will ask what I can do to make things better and I will act better, too," he decided. This would help him in his new life.

"I've made my list and I am willing," Billy announced. "If I have to swallow my pride, I will. If I have to take this fear by the hand, I will," Billy thought.

Yes, indeed, this was a very important list.

Now Billy knew that it was true.

Step Eight Follow-Up

Some lists are very important. The most important list Billy made included the pencils he had harmed. Making a list may seem simple. The difficult part is being willing to make amends.

• Have you ever hurt someone and tried to make things better?

_____

_____

• Did you ever struggle to make an apology?

_____

_____

_____

_____

Maybe you broke something that was not yours. Perhaps you called someone a name. When you saw how it hurt their feelings, you wished you could take it back. Sometimes saying 'I'm sorry' is not enough. We need to do more. For example, if you break someone's toy, it's best to fix or replace it. This is the meaning behind 'making amends'. It takes courage to be willing to do something like this.

An alcoholic has to set right any wrongs to keep sober. They make amends because they care and it gives them peace.

• Have you been hurt?
_____
_ _
_____

• Has anyone ever tried to make amends to you?
_____
_ _
_____

• How did it make you feel?
_____
_ _
_____
_____
_ _
_____

Step Nine
Made direct amends to such people except when to do so would injure them or others.

In many ways, Daniel was like all the other little bunnies of the world. But, in several other ways, he was quite different. One difference was that Daniel lived in a special cage. This cage changed quite often.

At times, it appeared to grow large but most of the time, it felt entirely too small for him. "I sure do wish I was through with this caged life," Daniel would often sigh. "I'd sure like to be free."

Daniel had something else that made him different, too. He could not seem to live in the present. Sometimes he would worry about the future. He'd worry and fret, "Oh, dear, what if this or that happens?"

Most of what he worried about never actually happened.

While he wasted some time worrying about these future situations, most of his time was spent thinking about the past. In his mind, Daniel would relive unpleasant events that happened in his life. "If Charlie didn't do that, I would be happy," and he believed it. "If Angie had only done this, I wouldn't be mad," he pouted. The fault was never his own.

Daniel remembered times when he felt hurt or angry. He remembered when he felt sad or guilty. All these feelings took place in the cage where he lived. When he finally came out to play, he was not much fun to play with. At times, he was downright difficult to be around.

Daniel knew he did not feel the happiness and peace that he wanted for himself and the pure joy that he observed others enjoying.

But, Daniel had been working on changing himself. He had gotten help from his friends and support from his God. He had gathered much courage and strength. More than anything, he wanted to correct the things he had said and done to hurt others. He looked at how his words and behavior had made the other bunnies feel.

As his mind cleared, he got a picture in his head. He thought of the times when he had gotten to play with others on the bunny playground. "It's like I've been on a see-saw all by myself," he realized. "Getting centered on a see-saw is impossible. I keep tipping from one side to the other."

Before he knew it, the see-saw had gone out of control and slammed to the ground. He had been hurt. "But, I realize now that the other bunnies had been hurt, too. We never got to play together because I was selfish."

"Enough of that!" he declared. "That's no way to live."

In his heart he knew, "I don't want to stay in my cage by myself. I want to be a bunny who can play nicely with other bunnies."

Although it took time, Daniel was confident that he could talk with the others and mend some of the hurts he had caused.

"Yes, this is what I need to do," he crinkled his nose and thought. "Maybe I can't fix everything, but I can admit to *my* part in it all."

At first he hoped, "Maybe I can just say I'm sorry." But his new best friend explained, "That's a good start, but you need to do more. You can do more by showing you are sorry and acting differently."

His friends called it "making amends". They said he'd be doing his part to set things right. They continued, "You don't have to beg. Just be sincere and open."

Daniel was more than a little nervous. "I'm not sure how things will go. Maybe they won't forgive me," he dreaded.

They offered more advice. "Try not to plan how it will turn out."

Daniel gathered all the courage he could muster and went on his way.

Not only did he say he was sorry, but he also admitted his faults. He even asked the most important question of all. "What can I do to make things right between us?"

As he started to make these "amends" he noticed a change. He stepped out of his cage and got a taste of the freedom he had been longing for. "This amends business isn't always easy but it sure is worth it!"

No longer caged like a trapped animal, now he was released. "What a relief!" He let go of the past and came back to the present. He felt very strange, yet very good. His mind grew clearer and his heart was lighter.

Now Daniel felt something new. Wings: tiny, dainty, and feathery wings. "My goodness," Daniel's eyes grew wide. First he drifted up like a balloon ever so safe and gentle. Then he flew the flight of angels. He felt a joy and freedom he had never known before.

Daniel had broken from the past. "What a glorious feeling!" he exclaimed. He no longer worried about the future either. "Oh my," his soul sighed with relief.

By making amends to the other bunnies, Daniel could feel the change and the healing. Sometimes simple things are grand like that.

Now Daniel knew that it was true.

Step Nine Follow-Up

At first, Daniel felt quite cramped in his cage. After he made his amends, he broke free and felt much happier. People call it 'cleaning their side of the street'.

When an alcoholic does the right thing they feel good because they can look people in the eye and no longer feel ashamed. No matter how the others respond, they know they did the right thing. It is a very important part of their recovery. After they have done this, they feel lighter and freer.

We cannot force people to forgive us, but we can do our best to correct our own behavior.

• Has someone you have known tried to make amends with you?

_____

- -

_____

_____

- -

_____

• How did you feel after they apologized?

_____

_ _

_____

_____

_ _

_____

• Was there something more that the person could have said or
  done?

_____

_ _

_____

_____

_ _

_____

Step Ten
Continued to take personal inventory and when we were wrong promptly admitted it.

Shelly was an extra special sea turtle. She had big, blue eyes and an olive green shell. As Shelly swam in the deep, open sea, she had one big wish; to grow up. After all, she was going to be a "Momma"!

Uncle Ridley often boasted he was almost fifty. If all went well, Shelly would have a long and happy life, too. At least she'd already come through the "Lost Years".

Even though she was ten years old, some days she still acted like a baby. When she didn't get her way, she would pout and frown. It was not a pretty sight. When she smacked the other turtles with her front flippers, they would say, "Shelly, don't be so mean!"

Her friends called her selfish when she gobbled up all the jellyfish. That wasn't acting very grown up. Wanting to be grown up and acting grown-up were not the same thing. She was old enough that she should have seen the difference. She had to let go of her selfish ways.

Shelly wanted to keep only her best behavior. "I only have so much space in my shell. I don't want to waste any." To be squished and cranky was no fun. "And selfish ways make me very cranky," she admitted to herself.

Life was easier and she felt better when she acted more grown-up. "Still, sometimes I know I'll make mistakes." Shelly knew no one was perfect.

Her big sister, Ava, had shown her the way to look at her own behavior. She called it "taking inventory". She explained, "Whether you do inventory or not is up to you." Ava also said, "Since the days of dinosaurs, turtles just like us have learned this habit and have had good results."

Friends along the way gave Shelly encouragement, too. They said, "Spend a few moments each day looking at your behavior. This is the way for you to make good progress."

Shelly thought, "Every day? Yikes!"

"Yes," said Ava. "You need to do the work on both good days and bad."

"How can that be?" Shelly wondered.

Finally, the day came when Shelly understood.

She had come out of the water to lay her eggs on the beach. The air was warm and her mind was fairly quiet. She had sat in this very spot before. As she nestled down in the sand to take a nap, she suddenly noticed how much the space had changed.

"What has happened to my special spot?" she wondered. Then she remembered. Her turtle schoolteacher had shown the class a picture of this very thing. Mrs. Snappy had called it "erosion".

"My special place has shrunk!" Shelly cried. "All the in and out movement of the waves must have done that." Yes, the constant moving of the tide had definitely changed the shoreline.

Mrs. Snappy had explained how erosion usually took a long time. "Well, I haven't been to my special spot for a whole year," Shelly recalled. "Boy that sure is a long time!"

After she settled in again, she put it together. "I will change like that too, slowly over time, like the shoreline. It won't happen all at once, but I know God and my friends will help me." She would continue to look at her behavior. "I might not notice at first, but over time I know I will change for the better." Shelly knew the truth, right down through her heart-shaped shell.

"I'll do my part to become what God wants me to be." Yes, she would keep "taking inventory" and setting right any new mistakes she made along the way. Change was not an overnight matter. Shelly was aware. "I'll need to work on this for my whole life."

Shelly floated off to sleep with peace in her heart and thoughts of her blessings. As she continued to take her own inventory, she would learn about true love for herself, her fellow turtles, and all of God's creatures. "These must be the good results Ava told me about," she sighed.

Using this inventory practice, she just might grow up.

Now Shelly knew that it was true.

Step Ten Follow-Up

Shelly wanted to grow up and be the best turtle she could be. To do this, she had to look at her behavior each day. Every evening before she went to sleep, Shelly used Ava's suggestion and took inventory. She looked back over her day.

Like Shelly, alcoholics in recovery do not do this just once. They continue to ask themselves some very important questions:

- Was I kind and loving to everyone?
- Have I kept something to myself that should be discussed at once?
- Was I thinking about how I could help others?
- Do I owe an apology when I see that I am wrong?
- What could I have done better?

These are all questions an alcoholic must ask himself every day. This practice helps them not drink.

- Before you go to sleep, do you ever look back over your day?

_____

_____

_____

_____

• Have you had your feelings hurt or did you hurt someone else's feelings?

_____

– –

_____

_____

– –

_____

• If so, what do you try to do about it?

_____

– –

_____

_____

– –

_____

Step Eleven
Sought through prayer and meditation to improve our conscious contact with God as we understood Him, praying only for the knowledge of his will for us and the power to carry that out.

Devon stood tall and alone in the meadow, grazing on tender young leaves. Her coat was golden brown with large, white spots. Her oversized ears helped her pick up sounds that the other deer missed.

Each day, the little fawn walked down a narrow trail in the early morning mist with the rest of the herd. Together they entered into the stillness.

One morning during this special quiet time, Devon heard a voice as soft as a whisper. An angel of God explained, "Your plans for the day are small compared to God's."

"How strange," she flicked her ears. "I've never considered what kind of plans God might have for me."

Devon knew about plans. There were little plans and big plans. She'd had them both. Usually Devon forced her plans to happen, instead of just letting them happen on their own.

She had a long to-do list swirling around in her head, but Devon didn't spend much time thinking of how to *BE* in the world.

"How will I ever learn how to listen for God's will?" she worried aloud.

Devon turned to her friend, Mary, who told her, "Everything takes practice, Devon, like swimming across the river or hiding during deer season. Only by practice, can hard things become easy," she assured her. "And before long, you'll begin to seek God's will. In fact, you won't want to do without prayer any more than you do without air, or food, or sunshine."

"So begin today," Mary instructed. "Even seeking God's will has a reward. You don't have to figure out a way to get to God, just let God find His way to you, Devon. The most important goal is to be still in your body and your mind. During the day if you are not sure what to do, stop and ask. The right thoughts or actions will be clear. If you practice, the right answers will come."

So, Devon began to practice. She closed her amber eyes to take in the silence. Every morning, she spent time seeking the will of God. "Boy, does this feel good," Devon exhaled.

The stillness was refreshing. She took it as a sure sign that she had contacted God. Devon learned to relax into her own skin right down to her hooves. She slowly began to take her life easy. "Why, I feel a little taller and a lot stronger," she couldn't help notice.

She stood alone in the meadow and listened to the birds singing and the hum of early morning traffic in the far distance. She saw clouds drift by in their ever-changing beauty and felt the soft breeze on her face. All this assured her of a higher purpose.

Devon exhaled and relaxed. "I don't have to know it all, just my part." She got still enough to hear the sounds of joy. She felt peace. Best of all, she knew there was love in the world. Her heart opened like a flower.

Even when life got hard, she remembered to be still. Devon learned to rely on God in more moments of each day. And all for the asking, she was given guidance and power. Whatever she needed was provided. At times, she needed encouragement and comfort. Most of the time she needed support and love.

In the stillness, Devon felt brand new, like the spring. And she knew a thing or two about spring. Spring began way down in the ground long before it could be seen in the world. Silence was the part of her the other deer could not see.

Her happiness began way down inside of her and came from God.

By praying and staying still, it was so clear that God's will was for her to be happy.

Now Devon knew that it was true.

Step Eleven Follow-Up

Devon had to learn to pray daily so she could hear God's plans for her. She had to seek God's will. There are a few ways people seek God's will. It's often said that prayer is a way of talking with God and meditation is a way of listening to God. Most people feel closer to God when they kneel down and close their eyes to pray.

• Is prayer a part of your daily life?

_____

_ _

_____

To feel God's presence, Devon had to be still. Stillness helped her be aware and brought her more peace than she had ever known.

• Do you ever enjoy being still?

_____

_ _

_____

Alcoholics practice staying close to God all day. It prevents them from being caught up in the rush of life. As they stay close to God, they are led toward their greatest good. They are led to do the 'next right thing'.

• What does this mean to you?

_____

- -

_____

_____

- -

_____

• Are you ever unsure of whether you are doing the next right
  thing?

_____

- -

_____

• If so, what helps you decide?

_____

- -

_____

_____

- -

_____

Step Twelve
Having had a spiritual awakening as a result of these steps, we tried to carry this message to others and practice these principles in all our affairs.

Sahara was a full-grown camel. His feet were wide and flat. These gave him a solid foundation and kept him from sinking in the sand. Life as a camel was not easy. Sahara had trekked many miles in his time. Work in the hot dry desert was hard, but he was tough.

Like the two humps on his back, Sahara had two important goals for his life.

His first goal was to carry a message. Sahara was built just right to carry people and heavy loads to places without roads, so this was right up his alley. But this time, he finally had something even more important to carry; a message of hope.

Earlier in his life, Sahara had spent years off by himself feeling lonely and unhappy. He had a sickness that would not go away. It centered in his mind. It did not get better. It only got worse.

He told his new friends, "I was so sure I could do everything myself. It never crossed my mind to rely on anyone else. I did not know how to accept help."

"I suffered in every way. My body hurt, my heart hurt, even my thoughts were scrambled. I was drifting with no anchor. I had no connection to God."

"I had a lot of self-pity. I was mad and I stayed sad all the time."

The moment he became willing to take suggestions from others, his solution came. "What a surprise," he marveled.

He realized he might help others find a way out of their suffering by sharing what happened to him. "By asking for help, I have healed."

"You can be free and you can be happy," he promised. "You can get well. That's the story I'll tell."

One story he loved to tell, showed just how this happened for him. "I had spent years off by myself," he told them.

"Yes," he claimed, "I survived, but only barely. Why I nearly died before I joined them."

"You see," he went on. "Once, not long ago, I had been stranded in the desert for many days.Times were tough, but I didn't imagine they could be any different."

Sahara continued, "The herd already knew if they clustered together, they could remain cool. Together their body temperatures were lower than the air's temperature."

"Finally, I saw the truth. I had to rely on them if I wanted to survive.This was one of the most important lessons in my life," he announced.

The others listened to Sahara's story without moving. No one said a word. Sahara smiled, "And we have stayed connected to each other long after we reached safety. In fact, we are lifelong friends."

"We are still learning more life lessons from each other." From the herd he began to understand about kindness, love, and tolerance for each other.

Sahara stood tall. "Together a group can do what a single camel alone cannot do. We can get better together."

Sahara's second goal was as important as his first. He needed to take what he had learned and use it in his new life each and every day.

Ever since the first day of his transformation, he learned so much more about himself and what he needed. He took the steps they suggested. "If I wanted to get better, I had to change." He noticed how each lesson fit together like the pieces of a puzzle.

He listened carefully when the other camels gathered. They explained to him in a way he understood, "When we make our dinner, Sahara, all of the ingredients are added in the proper order for our meal to be delicious. But, what we include now isn't the regular type like wheat, oats, and grass."

"Our ingredients are more important than what goes into our normal meals. We add ingredients like honesty, faith, and courage. These are worth having and extra yummy. And best of all, our recipe creates something wonderful and life changing."

The other camels supported him in his new life. Like a tree branch for a swing, they were sturdy and steady.

They told him, "Sahara, please remember this. You can do it. You can get better. All changes come 'little by little'. One day you'll look back and discover how far you've come. Just practice using these ingredients a little every day!"

And practice he did. Each day he became stronger and more grounded.

Sahara shared whatever he learned to help other camels make their lives better, too. This act was called service. Sahara liked to call it 'the gold'.

"Of all the ingredients I've learned about, it is without a doubt the most delicious," he smiled and snorted.

He encouraged them by sharing about himself. "I am like an acorn-seed growing into a mighty oak tree."

Somebody once called camels a name that Sahara liked. The name was, "Ship of the Desert". Camels moved across the desert sand, rocking back and forth like a boat in the sea. This was true of all camels, but finally Sahara realized his ship needed a rudder to be steered in the right direction. For him, that rudder was God.

"I hope it's like that for you as well," he said.

And best of all, he believed with all his heart, with God and his new found friends that his life would continue to be wonderful! He believed them when they said, "Our lives keep getting better and better."

"If we stay together, your life will continue to improve, too."

Now Sahara knew that it was true.

Step Twelve Follow-Up

After Sahara had a change in his personality, he understood he had a new purpose in his life that made him happy. He had to carry a message to other camels with the disease of alcoholism. This helped all of them get better together.

Alcoholics seek out and are available to help others in need. Even if they aren't sure they can do it, they try. Even if the others don't listen, it helps the alcoholic stay sober.

Alcoholics live by a new set of rules in their daily life. They are an example to others.

• What are some things that you do to help others?

_____

_ _

_____

_____

_ _

_____

• How does helping others make you feel?

_____

- -

_____

_____

- -

_____

Sahara made many new friends because he offered to help other camels feel better.

• Have you ever made new friends after helping someone?

_____

- -

_____

_____

- -

_____

Books for Kids

Alateen-Hope for Children of Alcoholics. 1600 Corporate Landing Pkwy, Virginia Beach, VA: 23454 Al-Anon Family Group Headquarters, Inc. www.alateen.org

Alcohol: What It Is, What It Does. Seixas, Judith S. Greenwillow Books, New York, NY, 1979.

An Elephant in the Living Room: Hastings & Typpo; Hazelden.

The Beamer Series. Tom Drennon and Jerry Moe. Rancho Mirage, California: Betty Ford Center, 2008. Beamer faces many challenges due to addiction in his family. In this series of four booklets, each containing three chapters, Beamer learns that he's not alone and addiction is not his fault. www.bettyfordcenter.org

Bottles Break. Nancy María Grande Tabor Watertown, MA: Charlesbridge Publishing, 1999. This book is about parents who are absorbed in drinking and how the young narrator feels about it. Included are helpful websites, addresses, and phone numbers. Also available in Spanish, Botellas Se Rompe.

The Brown Bottle. Penny James, Hazelden, 1983.

The Children's Place. At the Heart of Recovery, Jerry Moe and Ross Ziegler, 1998.

Daddy Doesn't Have To Be A Giant Anymore. Thomas, Jane Rest, Clarion Books, New York, NY, 1996.

Dear Kids of Alcoholics. Hall, Lindsey and Leigh Cohn, Gurze Books, Carlsbad, CA, 1988.

Don't Hurt Me, Mama. Stanek, Muriel, Albert Whitmen, and Co., Niles, IL, 1983.

Drugs, What They Are, What They Do. Seixas, Judith S. Greenwillow Books, New York, NY, 1987.

Emmy's Question. Jeannine Auth. St. Augustine, Florida: Morningtide Press, 2007. This is the powerful story of a young girl's struggle with parental alcoholism.

I Can Talk About What Hurts. Sinberg, Janet and Dennis Daley, Hazelden Publishing Center City, MN, 1993.

I Wish Daddy Didn't Drink So Much. Vigna, Judith, Albert Whitman and Co., Niles, IL.

Kids' Power Too! Words To Grow By. Cathey Brown, Elizabeth D'Angelo LaPorte and Jerry Moe.Dallas, TX:ImaginWorks.2010. A book of daily affirmations to help children, one day at a time, to face life's daily challenges in a healthy and balanced way.

Kit for Kids, booklet by the National Association for Children of Alcoholics, available at http://www.nacoa.org/prods.html.

Liking Myself, 3rd Edition. Palmer, Pat, Boulden Publishing, Weaverville, CA, 2011.

My Dad Loves Me, My Dad has a Disease. Claudia Black. Bainbridge Island, WA: MAC. 3rd Edition, Revised 2011. A workbook designed to help young children learn about themselves, their feelings, and the disease of alcoholism in their families through art therapy. Children between the ages of six and fourteen share what it is like for them to live in an alcoholic family.

My House Is Different: Kathie DiGiovanni; Hazelden Information Education, 1989.

National Association for Children of Alcoholics (NACoA)10920 Connecticut Ave, Suite 100 Kensington, MD 20895 1-888-554-COAS www.nacoa.org/kidspagehtml.

Sometimes My Mom Drinks Too Much. Kenny, Kevin and Helen Krull, Raintree Children's Books, Milwaukee, WI, 1980.

Think of Wind. Catherine Mercury. Rochester, NY: One Big Press, 1996. A book about how it feels for a child living with alcoholism in the family.

The Mouse, the Monster and Me: Assertiveness for Young People, 3rd Edition. Palmer, Pat, Boulden Publishing, Weaverville, CA, 2011.

Understanding Addiction and Recovery Through a Child's Eyes, Hope, Help, and Healing for Families, Jerry Moe, M.A., Health Communications, HCIbooks.com, 2007.

Up and Down the Mountain. Higgins, Pamela Leib, Small Horizons. Liberty Corner, NJ, 1995.

Welcome Home: A Child's View of Alcoholism. Jance, Judith, CharlesFranklinPress, Edmonds,WA,1986.

What's Drunk, Mama?: Al-Anon family Group Headquarters; Hazelden, 1977.

Parent Resources

Al–Anon Family Group Headquarters
Phone: (757) 563-1600 or (888) 425-2666
Internet address: www.al–anon.alateen.org
Makes referrals to local Al-Anon Groups. Provides locations of Al-Anon or Alateen meetings.

Alcoholics Anonymous (AA) World Services
Phone: (212) 870–3400
Internet address: www.aa.org
Makes referrals to local AA groups and provides informational materials on the AA program. Many cities and towns also have a local AA office listed in the telephone book.

NA.org (NA) World Service
Phone: (818) 773-9999
Internet address: www.na.org
Provides informational material on the NA programs. Locations of meetings can be obtained. Many cities and towns also have a local NA office listed in the telephone book.

NarAnon
Phone: (800) 477-6291
Internet address: www.nar-anon.org
Provides informational material on the NarAnon program. Locations of meetings can be obtained. Many cities and towns also have a local NarAnon office listed in the telephone book. Help for families and friends of drug addicts.

National Association for Children of Alcoholics (NACoA)
Phone: (888) 554-COAS or (301) 468–0985
E–mail: nacoa@nacoa.org
Internet address: www.nacoa.net
Works on behalf of children of alcohol and drug–dependent parents.

National Council on Alcoholism and Drug Dependence (NCADD)
Phone: (800) 622–2255
Internet address: www.ncadd.org
Provides telephone numbers of local NCADD affiliates (who can provide information on local treatment resources) and educational materials on alcoholism via the above toll–free number.

National Institute on Alcohol Abuse and Alcoholism (NIAAA)
Phone: (301) 443–3860
Internet address: www.niaaa.nih.gov
Makes available free publications on all aspects of alcohol abuse and alcoholism. Many are available in Spanish. Call, write, or search the NIAAA Web site for a list of publications and ordering information.

The National Center on Addiction and Substance Abuse at Columbia University
Phone: (212) 841-5200
Internet address: www.casacolumbia.org
Dedicated to changing the way America thinks about addiction.

The Partnership at DrugFree.org
Phone: (212) 922-1560
Internet address: www.drugfree.org
Working toward a vision where all young people will be able to live their lives free of drug or alcohol abuse.

Image Credits and More

A heartfelt thank you to my delightful new friend, Kristin Staats, who not only designed the cover, but captured my vision with her charming and unique graphic images. Above and beyond that, she shared my work with her charming mother, Kathy Staats, who proofread my stories with an unmatched level of care and commitment. Thank you both for helping this book come to life for me.

For more information and FREE downloadable workbook, visit my website at: www.12steps12stories.com

Thank you for taking the time to read my book.

I would appreciate it if you would make a review of my book. To create a review, follow the instructions below:
1. **Go to http://amazon.com**
2. **In the search block type 12 Steps 12 Stories**
3. **Double click on my book**
4. **On the right hand side click (# customer reviews)**
5. **Click to create your own review**

Made in the USA
Columbia, SC
16 December 2018